MISHA HABIB

A Beginner's Guide to Smart Living with AI

6 Easy Steps to Save Time and Money with Artificial Intelligence

This book was professionally typeset on Reedsy.
Find out more at reedsy.com

Contents

Introduction

I magine waking up on a Monday morning to the sound of your alarm. You reach for your phone, and with a simple voice command, your digital assistant begins to organize your day. Your emails are sorted, your meetings are scheduled, and even your breakfast order is placed—all before you've gotten out of bed.

Later, while driving to work, your AI-powered navigation system finds the quickest route through traffic, saving you precious minutes. At the office, AI manages your emails, prioritizes your calendar, and reminds you of important meetings. By the end of the day, you've saved hours of time and energy. This isn't a scene from a Sci-Fi movie; it's what living with Artificial Intelligence (AI) can be, and it's available to you right now.

Welcome to "A Beginner's Guide to Smart Living with AI: 6 Easy Steps to Save Time and Money with Artificial Intelligence." This book is designed to be a practical guide, equipping you with information to design a life that allows you more freedom and peace of mind. Whether you are new to AI or looking to deepen your understanding, this manual provides easy-to-follow instructions to help you lay the foundations of a life that is both supported and empowered through the use of AI.

As you move through the chapters you can start to incorporate AI tools into your routine immediately and begin to experience how Artificial Intelligence can unleash your ability to live smarter.

Why I Wrote This Book

There are things in life that intrigue and fascinate us. They might be the reason we spring out of bed every morning; things we feel are our reason for being; or perhaps even our purpose in life. Then there are things we feel we must do. Not necessarily things we want to do but things we know we must do. And there are successful people around the world that find ways to get up, show up and get these things done. But in between these two extremes are the things that quietly and nonchalantly enter our life and shape who we are and how we live. They are the things that happen to us and for us when we are busy making other plans.

This third category is how I define my relationship with Technology and AI. I can trace it all the way back to the 3rd grade when my school selected me as one of the students to take computer classes. And this was way back in the 1980's when desktops required a special air-conditioned computer lab.

I did not desire to or dream of becoming a computer scientist, nor was I compelled to study engineering like many South Asians of my generation were. I am not sure what convinced me to select this subject matter but I do remember how simple and straightforward studying Software Engineering and Information Systems was for me. Some of my fondest undergrad memories are of staying up late at night in the college computer labs as we cracked jokes and shared the stress as a team of students rummaging through our coding looking for the misplaced semicolons that were crashing our software.

My Masters in Information Systems and Management took me to The London School of Economics and to its classrooms and professors that opened my mind and world up to the absolute simplicity and brilliance of technology. Back when my Computer Science professors were still fascinated by the new concept of being able to write a letter on a computer and send it to anyone in the world for less than $0.01, I was sitting in classroom lectures of Globalization and Technology where we were being asked to imagine a world where a person can pick up a phone and call another person just by saying their name.

Over the years I have lived in 9 different cities over 3 continents. I have zigzagged between start-ups and large corporations, for profit and non-profit through industries that include Fashion, Real Estate, Retail and Agriculture. Through my work I was able to introduce IT innovations in the most interesting of spaces and places. And this was all before I moved to California's Silicon Valley where my relationship with technology and AI took on a whole new meaning.

Working in the Bay Area at Fortune 500 companies gave me the unique opportunity to work with some of the greatest technologies and minds in the field. I was not just a witness but an active participant of the overnight changes that Artificial Intelligence and Machine Learning were bringing to the world.

And no matter how technologically advanced or professionally intimidating the space has been, what has carried me through it all is that same reliable and safe relationship I have always had with Technology and AI. The quiet and nonchalant comfort I have when I put all my attention and focus on technology and its absolute simplicity and brilliance.

This book is my attempt to share the simplicity and brilliance of Technology and AI with you.

Vision for the Book

Have you heard the term, 'Don't work hard, work smart'? AI gives us the opportunity to apply this to our everyday life. We can all Live Smart with AI. As you work through these chapters my hope is you will start to shift from feeling overwhelmed and intimidated by AI to feeling both comfortable and empowered by it - laying the foundation to truly live a smart life.

Imagine AI as a set of futuristic looking building blocks. And you can use these blocks to build a lifestyle that provides you with far more freedom and peace of mind than you ever thought was possible. This book will introduce you to six basic AI building blocks, laying the foundation upon which you can architect and design an AI powered lifestyle that is tailor made for you by you.

Each chapter will introduce you to one building block or AI category and then get straight to the point; what is the AI category, examples of tools in that category, where can you access the tools from and how can you use them. The chapters also provide sample demos to support you in feeling comfortable to start using these tools right away. And if you require further assistance, you can also access links to the tool's help centers that can be found in the chapters and also in the reference section of this book. There's no fluff in these chapters—just the essential information you need to get started and make a significant impact on your efficiency and productivity.

Each chapter will also provide a breakdown of how the AI category can save you time and money. As you start to leverage AI to design a life to your specific needs and requirements, it is helpful to understand the many other ways the building block can benefit you. Which is why each chapter will also provide details of the other benefits each AI category can bring into your life.

These six categories are the basic building blocks of a smart life. As you incorporate these into your routine you will start to experience not just the simplicity and brilliance of these tools but also their synergy, because when woven into any lifestyle you will find they lead to profound exponential results.

My 20+ years of working has been an extraordinary journey of learning how people can incorporate technology to deliver efficiency, growth and innovation. I look forward to the opportunity to introduce you to technology and the world of AI through my eyes.

My goal is simple - to remove the confusion and fear around using Artificial Intelligence, specifically for people who have little to no experience with AI but are eager to leverage it to enhance their life.

I have often heard that a dog is a person's best friend. I also know one has to adjust to living with a dog before one starts to truly experience the joys of the relationship. AI is no different. Artificial Intelligence can be your most loyal companion once you begin to understand the art of living with AI.

I have been a writer for as long as I can remember. And more recently, AI has found ways to support me in this area of my life. Initially it was just my spell check, and now with tools like ChatGPT, it is proving to have the capacity to be so much more. Understanding technology's value in any area of one's life requires one to first accept the possibility and then slowly start to embrace its potential. That is what I am trying to do as I write this book for you with AI as my assistant. I am so excited to invite you to explore this new world of AI as we normalize it and befriend it in more and more aspects of our life.

What You Will Learn

Below is an overview of what you can expect to learn as you work your way through the pages of this book.

1. **Voice Activated Assistants**: Learn how to utilize voice-activated assistants like Siri, Google Assistant and Alexa for daily tasks such as setting reminders, checking the weather and playing music. Discover practical steps to set up and use these tools effectively.

2. **AI-Powered Email and Calendar Management**: Optimize your email and calendar management with AI features in services like Gmail and Microsoft Outlook. Understand how to set up filters to automatically sort emails into folders, use Smart Reply and Smart Compose to handle routine emails and manage your schedule efficiently with Outlook's scheduling assistant and Focused Inbox.

3. **AI-Powered Navigation**: Explore AI in navigation apps like Google Maps and Waze for real-time traffic updates and optimal route planning. Learn how ride-sharing services like Uber use AI for efficient ride matching and route optimization. Practical demos will guide you through setting up and using these tools to make travel smoother and more enjoyable.

4. **AI-Powered Financial Management**: Manage your finances with AI-powered apps like Mint and Wealthfront to create budgets,

track expenses and receive investment advice. Discover how to use Google Finance and Google Sheets for investment tracking and budgeting and how Apple Wallet can help manage digital payments and track spending.

5. **AI-Enabled Health and Fitness Apps**: Use AI-enabled apps like MyFitnessPal for tracking nutrition, Sleep Cycle for improving sleep patterns and fitness trackers like Fitbit or Apple Watch for monitoring physical activity. Learn how these tools can help you maintain a healthier lifestyle and achieve your fitness goals.

6. **AI Language Translation Tools**: Employ AI translation tools like Google Translate and Microsoft Translator for communicating in different languages. Understand how these tools can be particularly useful for travel or learning new languages, including features that translate text, speech and images in real-time.

These chapters will equip you with the knowledge and practical skills to integrate AI tools into your daily routine, helping you save time, reduce costs, increase productivity and improve your overall quality of life.

I hope building your smart life with AI is as enjoyable, enriching and profitable for you as Artificial Intelligence and Technology has always been for me.

Building Block 1: Voice Activated Assistants

Meet Lisa, a busy working mom juggling the demands of a full-time job, two kids and household responsibilities. Her work week can be an absolute whirlwind of chaos. A busy working mom requires support that feels safe, reliable and trustworthy. AI was able to provide that because once she began to leverage Siri, her days started to look very different.

Every morning, as soon as Lisa's alarm goes off, she simply says, "Hey Siri, good morning." Instantly, Siri responds with the weather forecast, her calendar appointments for the day and a quick news briefing. While Lisa gets ready, Siri sets reminders for her kids' school events and even orders groceries for delivery based on her preset shopping list.

On her commute to work, Lisa uses Siri to send hands-free texts, check traffic updates, and adjust her home's thermostat to save energy while she's away. By the time she arrives at the office, her day is more organized and she feels far more in control.

Lisa's use of Siri doesn't stop at work. She uses it to set reminders for meetings, draft emails using voice commands and even to schedule her coffee breaks. At home, Siri helps her manage her family's schedule, play music, and control smart home devices like lights and security systems.

Lisa's story illustrates the power of voice-activated assistants. These digital helpers can perform a wide range of tasks, from setting reminders to controlling smart home devices. In this chapter, we'll explore what voice assistants are, how they work, and how you can leverage them to simplify your daily routine.

What is a Voice Activated Assistant and Why Should I Have One?

A voice activated assistant is a category of digital tools that use natural language processing and machine learning to understand and respond to your voice commands. Popular examples include Siri (Apple), Google Assistant (Google), and Alexa (Amazon). They perform a variety of functions:

- **Information Retrieval**: It can provide answers about the weather, news, or general knowledge questions.
- **Task Management**: Set reminders, alarms and calendar events.
- **Entertainment**: Play music, podcasts or audio-books.
- **Smart Home Control**: Operate lights, thermostats and other smart devices.
- **Communication**: Send texts, make calls and read out notifications.

Voice activated assistants (or voice assistants) can make everyday tasks more manageable, allowing you to focus on more important activities.

How Do I Get One?

Getting a voice assistant is straightforward and often involves devices you may already own:

Siri: Available on Apple devices such as iPhones, iPads, Macs, and Apple Watches. Simply activate it by saying, "Hey Siri," or pressing the home button on your device.

- For details on Siri's setup refer to: https://support.apple.com/

Google Assistant: Found on Android devices and Google Home speakers. You can activate it by saying, "Hey Google" or "OK Google." It's also available through the Google Assistant app on iOS.

- For further details on Google Assistant Setup refer to: https://support.google.com/assistant/topic/

How Do I Use It?

Using a voice assistant is intuitive and requires minimal setup:

Basic Commands: Start with simple commands like asking for the weather, setting reminders, or playing music. For example:

- "Hey Siri, what's the weather today?"
- "OK Google, set a reminder for my meeting at 3 PM."
- "Hey Google, play my favorite playlist."

Customization: Customize your assistant to better fit your needs. For instance, you can create routines that trigger multiple actions with a single command. Example: "Good morning" can turn on the lights, read the news, and start your coffee maker.

How Can It Save Me Time and Money?

Here are some examples of how voice assistants can improve your efficiency and save you money:

- **Time Savings**: Studies show that using a voice assistant can save up to 30 minutes per day by automating routine tasks. Instead of manually searching for information or setting reminders, you can do it instantly with your voice.
- **Cost Savings**: By using voice assistants to control smart home devices, you can reduce energy consumption. For instance, setting your thermostat through a voice command can optimize heating and cooling, potentially saving up to 10% on energy bills annually.
- **Productivity**: Managing your calendar, setting reminders, and sending messages hands-free allows you to focus on more important tasks, thereby increasing your productivity.

How Else Can It Benefit Me?

Beyond saving time and money, voice assistants offer several additional benefits:

- **Health and Safety**: Voice assistants can remind you to take medications, schedule doctor appointments and even call for help in emergencies.
- **Entertainment**: They can play your favorite music, audio-books, and podcasts, or even tell you jokes and stories to keep you entertained.

- **Learning and Education**: Use them to learn new things by asking questions, translating languages, or even practicing new skills through guided tutorials.
- **Smart Home Integration**: Voice assistants can control smart home devices, such as lights, locks, and security cameras, enhancing your home's safety and convenience.

Practical Demo: Setting Up and Using Voice Activated Assistants

To help you get started, let's walk through a practical demo of setting up Siri and creating a shortcut, also known as a routine.

Setting Up Siri

Enable Siri: On your iPhone or iPad:

- Go to **Settings > Siri & Search**.
- Toggle on **Listen for "Hey Siri"** and **Press Side Button for Siri**.
- Follow the on-screen instructions to train Siri to recognize your voice.

Check Siri Settings:

- Ensure **Allow Siri When Locked** is turned on so you can use Siri without unlocking your device.
- Customize Siri's voice and language settings under **Siri Voice** and **Language**.

Link Apple ID:

- Make sure your device is signed in with your Apple ID to enable personalized Siri features. Go to **Settings > [Your Name]** and check if your Apple ID is signed in.

Creating a Shortcut (Routine)

Siri Shortcuts allow you to automate multiple actions with a single voice command. Here's how you can create a shortcut: (For further details on Shortcut setup refer to: https://support.apple.com/guide/)

Open Shortcuts App:

- On your iPhone or iPad, open the **Shortcuts** app. If you don't have it, you can download it from the App Store.

Create a New Shortcut:

- Tap the + icon in the top right corner to create a new shortcut.
- Tap **Add Action** to choose the first action in your shortcut. For example, you can add an action to play music, set a reminder, or get the weather.

Customize Your Shortcut:

- Add multiple actions to create a sequence. For example, you can create a morning routine that turns on the lights, reads your schedule, and plays your favorite music.
- Tap **Next** when you've added all desired actions.

Name Your Shortcut:

- Give your shortcut a name. This is the phrase you'll use to trigger the shortcut with Siri.

- Tap **Done** to save your shortcut.

Use Your Shortcut:

- Activate your shortcut by saying, "Hey Siri, [Shortcut Name]."

Example Shortcut: Morning Routine

- **Action 1**: Get the weather for today.
- **Action 2**: Read today's calendar events.
- **Action 3**: Play a specific playlist.

Voice-activated assistants are powerful tools that can make your daily life more efficient and enjoyable. By understanding what they are, how to get one, and how to use them, you're well on your way to integrating AI into your routine. Next, we'll explore AI-powered email and calendar management to help you stay organized and on top of your tasks. Get ready to take control of your schedule with the help of AI!

Building Block 2: AI-Powered Email and Calendar Management

Meet David, a middle-aged small business owner who runs a local bakery. David is not particularly tech-savvy and prefers to spend his time perfecting recipes rather than managing emails and schedules. His mornings used to start with sifting through a cluttered inbox and trying to remember important meetings and deliveries. That was until he discovered AI-powered email and calendar management tools.

David began using Gmail to help manage his daily communications. The Smart Reply and Smart Compose features quickly became his go-to tools for handling routine emails. With AI suggesting responses and completing his sentences, David could swiftly reply to customer inquiries and supplier communications, giving him more time to focus on baking.

To keep his inbox organized, David set up filters that automatically sorted incoming emails. For instance, orders from customers went straight into an "Orders" folder, while newsletters and promotional emails were moved to a "Marketing" folder. This simple change helped David stay on top of his priorities without feeling overwhelmed by the volume of emails.

David also embraced Gmail's calendar features for his scheduling needs. The integration of Google Calendar allowed him to effortlessly set up and manage his appointments. David used the smart scheduling feature to find the best times for meetings with suppliers and staff, eliminating the back-and-forth email chains. With the Focused Inbox feature, David could easily prioritize urgent emails, ensuring he never missed an important message.

The transformation didn't stop at email management. With AI managing his calendar, David received timely reminders about upcoming deliveries, staff schedules and even personal appointments. This new level of organization allowed David to run his bakery more efficiently, reducing stress and improving customer satisfaction.

David's story shows how AI-powered email and calendar management tools can be a game-changer, even for those who are not tech-savvy. Let's dive into the details of how you can leverage these tools to optimize your email and calendar management.

What is AI-Powered Email and Calendar Management and Why Should I Use It?

Email and calendar management involves organizing, prioritizing and handling your emails and schedules efficiently. Integrating AI into these tasks can make the process seamless and automated, allowing you to focus on more important activities. Here's why you should consider using AI-powered email and calendar management:

- **Efficiency**: Quickly sort, respond and schedule without manual

effort.
- **Organization**: Keep your inbox and calendar clutter-free and well-organized.
- **Productivity**: Automate routine tasks to free up time for more significant work.

How Do I Get It?

Most modern email and calendar services come with built-in AI features. Here's how you can access some of the popular options:

Gmail: Gmail's AI features, like Smart Reply and Smart Compose, are available to all users. These tools suggest replies and help you write emails faster.

- For further details go to: Gmail or https://support.google.com/

Microsoft Outlook: Outlook's scheduling assistant and focused inbox are available to users with a Microsoft 365 subscription.

- For further details go to: Microsoft Outlook or https://www.micr osoft.com/

How Do I Use It?

Using AI features in your email and calendar applications is straightforward:

Gmail's Smart Reply and Smart Compose:

Smart Reply: When you receive an email, Gmail suggests quick responses based on the content of the email.

- Open an email and look at the suggested replies at the bottom.
- Tap on a suggested reply to use it.

Smart Compose: While typing an email, Gmail suggests phrases to complete your sentences.

- Start typing an email, and look for grayed-out text suggestions.
- Press the tab key to accept a suggestion.

Microsoft Outlook's Scheduling Assistant and Focused Inbox:

Scheduling Assistant: Helps you find the best time for meetings.

- Open the calendar in Outlook.
- Create a new event and add attendees.
- Click on "Scheduling Assistant" to see the availability of all attendees.

Focused Inbox: Separates important emails from the rest.

- Enable Focused Inbox from the settings menu.
- Emails are automatically sorted into "Focused" and "Other" tabs.

How Can It Save Me Time and Money?

AI-powered email and calendar management tools can significantly improve your efficiency and save you time and money. Here's how:

- **Time Savings**: AI features like Smart Reply can reduce the time spent on emails by up to 50%. For example, quick replies eliminate the need to type out common responses manually.
- **Productivity**: By automating meeting scheduling, the scheduling assistant can save hours each week that would otherwise be spent coordinating times with colleagues.
- **Cost Savings**: Improved productivity means less time spent on mundane tasks, allowing you to focus on higher-value activities, which can lead to cost savings in a business context.

How Else Can It Benefit Me?

Beyond saving time and money, AI-powered email and calendar management offers several additional benefits:

- **Reduced Stress**: Automatically sorting emails and suggesting replies can reduce the mental load associated with managing a busy inbox.
- **Improved Organization**: Features like Focused Inbox keep your important emails front and center, ensuring you don't miss critical information.
- **Enhanced Collaboration**: Scheduling assistants make it easier to coordinate with colleagues, improving team collaboration and meeting efficiency.

Practical Demo: Setting Up and Using AI-Powered Email and Calendar Features

To help you get started, let's walk through a practical demo of setting up and using AI-powered email and calendar features in Gmail:

Enable Smart Reply and Smart Compose:

- Open Gmail and go to Settings (gear icon) > See all settings.
- In the "General" tab, scroll to "Smart Reply" and "Smart Compose" and make sure both are turned on.

Creating a Folder and Filter in Gmail:
Create a New Label:

- Open Gmail and go to the left sidebar.
- Scroll down and click on **More**.
- Click on **Create new label**.
- Name your new label (e.g., "Work", "Important").

Create a Filter:

- Click on the search bar at the top of the Gmail interface.
- Click on the dropdown arrow to open advanced search options.
- Enter the criteria for the filter (e.g., emails from a specific sender or containing certain keywords).
- Click on **Create filter** at the bottom of the search window.
- Choose what you want the filter to do (e.g., Skip the Inbox, Apply the label "Work").
- Check the box next to **Apply the label** and select your newly created label from the drop-down menu.

- Click on **Create filter** to finalize.

AI-powered email and calendar management tools are powerful resources that can streamline your daily routines and enhance productivity. By taking the time to understand what they are and how you can utilize them, you can integrate these tools into your workflow with ease.

Building Block 3: AI-Powered Navigation

Meet Nava, Mark, David, and Deepak, four individuals with different lifestyles and travel needs who have revolutionized their travel experiences using AI-powered navigation systems.

Nava, an avid solo traveler from the United States, decided to visit Tokyo, Japan. Although she was excited about exploring the city, she was also apprehensive about navigating through Tokyo's complex transportation system and language barrier. To ease her travel experience, Nava relied heavily on Google Maps. She used the app to navigate Tokyo's extensive subway system, receive real-time updates on train schedules, and explore local attractions. Nava also downloaded offline maps to avoid international data charges, ensuring she never got lost while exploring the city. Her use of Google Maps made getting around the city stress-free and efficient, allowing her to enjoy the exciting culture and sights of Tokyo without worrying about getting lost.

Mark, a freelance photographer who loves exploring new locations for his shoots, prefers Waze for its community-driven updates. On a sunny Saturday, Mark had a photo session in a remote countryside location. Using Waze, he entered his destination and was guided not only through the quickest routes but also scenic paths that offered beautiful landscapes. The app alerted him to unexpected road closures and police checks reported by other users, making his journey safer and more enjoyable. The real-time user contributions and detailed navigation helped Mark reach his destination efficiently and with peace of mind.

David, a middle-aged small business owner who runs a local bakery, uses AI tools to manage his hectic schedule. For navigation, David used Waze while traveling to Barcelona, Spain with his family. Renting a car to explore the city and its surroundings, Waze provided him with real-time traffic updates, road closures, and accident reports, helping him avoid traffic jams and find the fastest routes. The app also helped David locate available parking spots near popular tourist sites, saving him time and reducing the stress of searching for parking. Through Waze's user-generated content, David discovered lesser-known scenic routes and local eateries, enhancing his family's travel experience.

Deepak, a college student without a car, relies on Uber to get around the city. One Friday night, Deepak needed to get to a friend's birthday party across town. Instead of worrying about bus schedules or finding a taxi, he opened the Uber app, entered his destination, and requested a ride. Within minutes, a driver was on the way. The app calculated the best route, factoring in traffic conditions to ensure a quick trip. Uber's AI-powered system matched him with the nearest driver, optimizing route planning and reducing wait times. Deepak arrived at the party stress-free, appreciating the convenience and efficiency of the service.

These stories show how AI-powered navigation tools can transform both regular commutes and unique travel adventures. Travel becomes more efficient, safe, and enjoyable. Let's dive into how you can leverage these tools to optimize your navigation.

What is AI-Powered Navigation and Why Should I Use It?

AI-powered navigation involves using artificial intelligence to optimize travel routes, provide real-time traffic updates and enhance overall travel efficiency. These tools analyze vast amounts of data to make your journey smoother and more predictable. Here are some key reasons why you should consider using AI-powered navigation:

- **Real-Time Updates**: Receive instant updates on traffic conditions, road closures, and accidents.
- **Optimal Routes**: Get suggestions for the fastest or most efficient routes to your destination.
- **Efficiency**: Reduce travel time and fuel consumption, saving you money and reducing stress.

How Do I Get It?

Most modern smartphones come with built-in navigation apps that leverage AI. Here's how you can access and set up these features:

Google Maps: Available on both Android and iOS devices, Google Maps provides comprehensive navigation services.

- Link to Google Maps: https://www.google.com/maps

Waze: Also available on Android and iOS, Waze offers community-driven navigation with real-time traffic updates.

- Link to Waze: https://www.waze.com/live-map/

Ride-Sharing Apps: Uber uses AI to match riders with drivers efficiently.

- Link to Uber: https://www.uber.com/

How Do I Use It?

Using AI-powered navigation and ride-sharing services is straightforward. Here's a step-by-step guide:

Google Maps:

Set Up: Download and open the Google Maps app. Sign in with your Google account for personalized features.

Basic Navigation:

- Enter your destination in the search bar.
- Tap on "Directions" to see the suggested routes.
- Choose your preferred route and tap "Start" for turn-by-turn navigation.

Real-Time Traffic Updates: Google Maps will automatically provide traffic updates and suggest alternative routes if there are delays.

Waze

Set Up: Download and open the Waze app. Create an account or sign in.

Basic Navigation:

- Enter your destination in the search bar.
- Tap on "Go" to see the suggested routes.
- Waze will provide turn-by-turn navigation with real-time updates from other users.

Community Reports: Waze allows users to report traffic, accidents, and road hazards, which helps improve navigation accuracy.

Ride-Sharing Apps (Uber):

Set Up: Download and open the Uber app. Sign up or log in with your account.

Request a Ride:

- Enter your pickup location and destination.
- Choose your ride option (e.g., standard, shared, or luxury).
- Confirm your ride request and wait for a driver to be matched.

Ride Matching and Route Optimization: AI matches you with the nearest driver and calculates the best route to your destination.

How Can It Save Me Time and Money?

AI-powered navigation tools can significantly improve your travel efficiency and save you time and money. Here's how:

- **Time Savings**: By providing real-time traffic updates and suggesting optimal routes, AI navigation apps can reduce travel time by up to 20%. For instance, if there's a traffic jam ahead, these apps will reroute you to avoid delays.
- **Cost Savings**: Efficient route planning reduces fuel consumption, saving you money on gas. Additionally, ride-sharing apps often offer cost-effective shared ride options that are normally cheaper than traditional taxi services.
- **Productivity**: Spend less time on the road and more time on productive activities. For example, knowing the exact time of arrival allows you to plan your day better.

How Else Can It Benefit Me?

Beyond saving time and money, AI-powered navigation offers several additional benefits:

- **Reduced Stress**: Knowing the best routes and having real-time updates can reduce the anxiety associated with travel.
- **Safety**: Avoid dangerous areas and road hazards with real-time alerts from apps like Waze.
- **Environmental Impact**: Efficient route planning and ride-sharing contribute to reduced carbon emissions by minimizing unnecessary driving and encouraging carpooling.

Practical Demo: Setting Up and Using AI-Powered Navigation

To help you get started, let's walk through a practical demo of setting up and using AI-powered navigation features in Google Maps, Waze, and Uber:

Google Maps Setup:
   Enable Traffic Layer:

- Open Google Maps and tap on the 'layers' icon (three stacked lines).
- Select "Traffic" to enable real-time traffic updates.
- For Further details, go to: https://support.google.com/maps/

Waze Setup:
   Enable Traffic Reports:

- Open Waze and go to Settings > Reports.
- Ensure all report types (traffic, police, accidents) are enabled.

Using Uber:
   Requesting a Ride:

- Open the app and enter your pickup and drop-off locations.
- Select your ride type and confirm your request.
- For further support, here a link to Uber's startup guide: https://www.uber.com/us/en/ride/how-it-works/

AI-powered navigation and ride-sharing tools are powerful resources that can simplify your travel, reduce stress, and save you time and money. With a little practice, you can easily incorporate them into your routine and lifestyle.

Building Block 4: AI-Powered Financial Management

Meet Peter, Sabrina, and Zain—three individuals from diverse backgrounds who have transformed their financial management using AI-powered tools.

Peter, a married man with a wife and three kids, runs a small family-owned restaurant. Managing personal and business finances became overwhelming for Peter, who struggled to keep track of expenses, save for his children's education, and ensure his business stayed profitable. He discovered Mint, an AI-powered financial management app that simplified his finances. By linking all his bank accounts, credit cards, and loans, Mint automatically categorized his transactions and provided insights into his spending habits. Peter could set budgets for different categories, like groceries and utilities, and receive alerts when he was nearing his limits. With the help of Mint, Peter felt more in control of his finances, reduced unnecessary expenses, and set up a savings plan for his kids' future education.

Sabrina, a busy nurse who juggles long shifts and a demanding schedule, found it challenging to manage her finances effectively. She started using Wealthfront, an AI-driven financial advisor app. Wealthfront analyzed her income and spending patterns, helping her identify areas where she could save money. The app automatically invested her savings into a diversified portfolio based on her risk tolerance and financial goals. With Wealthfront's personalized financial planning and automated investment management, Sabrina quickly built an emergency fund and started saving for a down payment on a house. The app's real-time financial insights and automated investment strategies made it easier for Sabrina to achieve her financial goals without the hassle of manual tracking.

Zain, a freelance artist, manages multiple streams of income from various projects. He uses Google's financial tools to streamline his financial management. Google Sheets, integrated with Google Finance, helps Zain track his investments and monitor the stock market in real-time. By creating custom financial dashboards, he can visualize his income, expenses, and savings goals. Additionally, Zain utilizes Apple's Wallet app to manage his digital payments and keep track of his spending. With Apple Pay, he makes secure transactions and categorizes his purchases automatically. These tools provide Zain with a comprehensive view of his finances, enabling him to make informed decisions and optimize his earnings.

These stories highlight the transformative power of AI-powered financial management tools. Let's explore how you can leverage these tools to take control of your finances and achieve your financial goals.

What is AI-Powered Financial Management and Why Should I Use It?

AI-powered financial management involves using artificial intelligence to analyze your financial data, provide insights and automate tasks related to budgeting, expense tracking and investment. These tools can help you make better financial decisions by providing personalized recommendations and real-time updates. Here are some key reasons why you should consider using AI-powered financial management:

- **Automation**: Automatically categorize expenses, track spending, and create budgets.
- **Personalization**: Receive tailored advice based on your financial goals and behavior.
- **Efficiency**: Save time by automating routine financial tasks.

How Do I Get It?

Many AI-powered financial management tools are available as apps for smartphones or web platforms. Here's how you can access some popular options:

Mint: A free app that helps you manage your budget, track expenses, and monitor your credit score.

- For further info go to: Mint or https://mint.intuit.com/

Wealthfront: An app that helps you save money by analyzing your spending and income patterns and automatically investing into a diversified portfolio.

- For further info go to: Wealthfront or https://www.wealthfront.co m/

Google Finance and Google Sheets: Tools for tracking investments, creating budgets, and monitoring financial data.

- For further info go to: Google Finance or https://www.google.co m/finance/
- For more info on setting up Google sheets refer to: https://worksp ace.google.com/products/sheets/

Apple Wallet: A digital wallet for managing payments, tracking purchases, and making secure transactions.

- For further info go to: Apple Wallet or https://www.apple.com/ap ple-pay/

How Do I Use It?

Using AI-powered financial management tools is straightforward. Here's a step-by-step guide:
Mint:
Set Up: Download and open the Mint app. Create an account and link your bank accounts, credit cards, and other financial accounts.
Budgeting:

- Mint will automatically categorize your transactions and suggest budget categories.
- Customize your budget by adjusting categories and setting spending limits.

Expense Tracking:

- View your spending patterns and trends on the dashboard.
- Use alerts and reminders to stay on top of bills and due dates.

Wealthfront:

Set Up: Download and open the Wealthfront app. Create an account and complete the initial questionnaire to determine your risk tolerance and financial goals.

Automated Investing:

- Wealthfront will create a personalized investment portfolio based on your inputs.
- Link your bank account to start funding your investment account.

Financial Planning:

- Use Wealthfront's financial planning tools to set and track goals like retirement, buying a home or saving for college.

Google Finance and Google Sheets:
Investment Tracking:

- Use Google Finance to monitor stock market trends and track your investments.

- Create a custom financial dashboard in Google Sheets to visualize your income, expenses and savings goals.

Budgeting and Expense Tracking:

- Use Google Sheets templates to create budgets and track your expenses.

Apple Wallet:
Digital Payments:

- Use Apple Wallet to store your credit and debit cards for secure digital payments.
- Track your purchases and categorize expenses automatically.

Expense Management:

- Use the Wallet app to monitor your spending and manage subscriptions.

How Can It Save Me Time and Money?

AI-powered financial management tools can significantly improve your efficiency and save you time and money. Here's how:

- **Time Savings**: Automate routine tasks like expense tracking and budgeting, reducing the time spent on manual financial management.

- **Cost Savings**: Identify unnecessary expenses and areas for saving. For example, Mint can alert you to subscriptions you may have forgotten about or areas where you're overspending.
- **Investment Efficiency**: Robo-advisors and tools like Google Finance use algorithms to optimize your investment portfolio, potentially increasing returns and reducing fees compared to traditional financial advisors.

How Else Can It Benefit Me?

Beyond saving time and money, AI-powered financial management offers several additional benefits:

- **Financial Awareness**: Gain a clearer understanding of your financial situation with real-time data and insights.
- **Goal Setting and Tracking**: Set financial goals and track your progress, making it easier to achieve milestones like saving for a vacation or buying a house.
- **Stress Reduction**: Automating financial tasks and receiving personalized advice can reduce the stress associated with managing finances.

Practical Demo: Setting Up and Using AI-Powered Financial Management

To help you get started with AI-powered financial management, let's walk through the detailed steps of setting up and using features in Mint, Google Finance, and Apple Wallet.

Setting Up Mint
  Create an Account:

- Go to the Mint website or download the Mint app on your smartphone.
- Click on **Sign Up** and enter your email address, create a password and follow the prompts to create your account.

Link Financial Accounts:

- Once logged in, Mint will prompt you to link your bank accounts, credit cards, loans, and other financial accounts.
- Select your financial institution from the list and enter your login credentials to connect the account.
- Repeat this process for all the financial accounts you want to track in Mint.

Set Up Budgets:

- Go to the **Budgets** tab.
- Click on **Create a Budget**.
- Select a spending category (e.g., groceries, utilities) and set a spending limit for each category.

- Mint will automatically categorize your transactions and track your spending against these budgets.

Track Expenses:

- View your spending patterns and trends on the **Overview** dashboard.
- Use the **Transactions** tab to review all your transactions, categorized by Mint.
- Set up alerts and reminders for bills and budget limits.

Set Goals:

- Go to the **Goals** tab.
- Select a financial goal (e.g., saving for a vacation, paying off debt).
- Enter the goal amount and timeline and Mint will help you create a plan to achieve it.

Setting Up Google Finance and Google Sheets
Create a Google Account:

- If you don't have one already, create a Google account. For further info on how to create one, go to: https://support.google.com/

Set Up Google Finance:

- Go to Google Finance: https://www.google.com/finance/
- Use the search bar to look up stocks, bonds, and other financial assets you want to track.
- Click the **Follow** button to add them to your watchlist.

Create a Financial Dashboard in Google Sheets:

- Open Google Sheets and create a new spreadsheet.
- Use templates or create custom sheets to track your income, expenses, and investments.
- To link Google Finance data, use the GOOGLEFINANCE function. For example, =GOOGLEFINANCE("GOOG", "price") will display the current stock price for Google.

Track Investments:

- Input your investment details (e.g., stocks, mutual funds) in the spreadsheet.
- Use Google Finance functions to pull real-time data into your sheet.
- Create charts and graphs to visualize your investment performance and financial health.

Setting Up Apple Wallet
Add Cards to Apple Wallet:

- Open the Wallet app on your iPhone.
- Tap the + sign to add a new card.
- Follow the instructions to add your credit or debit card. You can either manually enter your card details or use your iPhone camera to scan the card.
- Your bank may require additional verification. Follow the prompts to complete this process.

Set Up Apple Pay:

- Once your card is added to Wallet, it will automatically be set up for Apple Pay.

- To make a payment, hold your iPhone near a contactless payment terminal with your finger on the Touch ID sensor or double-click the side button for Face ID.

Track Spending:

- Use the Wallet app to view recent transactions made with Apple Pay.
- Transactions will be categorized automatically, helping you keep track of your spending habits.

Manage Subscriptions:

- Go to **Settings > Your Name > Subscriptions**.
- View and manage your subscriptions, including canceling any services you no longer need.

By following these steps, you can begin to set up and use AI-powered financial management tools to gain a better understanding of your financial situation and make profitable decisions. You will find that integrating these tools into your daily routine will help you feel more in control and empowered over your finances.

Building Block 5: AI-Enabled Health and Fitness Apps

Meet Amanda, Mat, Rachel and Dan—four individuals with diverse lifestyles and fitness goals who have transformed their health routines using AI-powered health and fitness apps.

Amanda is a busy school teacher who struggles to maintain a healthy lifestyle a midst her hectic schedule. She discovered MyFitnessPal, an AI-enabled app that helps her track her nutrition effortlessly. By logging her meals, Amanda receives detailed nutritional information, which helps her make better food choices. Over time, she notices weight loss and increased energy levels, thanks to the insights provided by MyFitnessPal.

Mat is a partner at a law firm who used to have erratic sleep patterns that left him feeling exhausted. He decided to try Sleep Cycle, an AI-powered app designed to improve sleep quality. By placing his phone near his bed, the app analyzed his sleep patterns using sound and motion data. It provided personalized tips to enhance his sleep environment and habits. After a few weeks, Mat experienced more restful nights and more productive days.

Rachel, a retiree, wanted to ensure she stayed active and healthy. She started using Fitbit, an AI-enabled fitness tracker, to monitor her physical activity. The Fitbit app provided real-time data on her steps, heart rate, and calories burned. It also offered personalized workout recommendations based on her fitness goals. With Fitbit's detailed insights and motivation, Rachel saw significant improvements in her fitness levels and overall health.

Dan, a small business owner, struggled to find time for fitness. He turned to his Apple Watch to integrate health tracking seamlessly into his daily routine. The Apple Watch tracked his activity, reminded him to stand up regularly, and helped him meet his fitness goals through personalized workout suggestions. Dan found the convenience of having a fitness coach on his wrist invaluable, helping him stay active despite his busy schedule.

These stories highlight the transformative power of AI-enabled health and fitness apps. Let's explore how you can leverage these tools to enhance your health and well-being.

What is AI-Enabled Health and Fitness Apps and Why Should I Use Them?

AI-enabled health and fitness apps use artificial intelligence to analyze your health data, provide personalized recommendations and automate tracking processes. These tools can help you make informed decisions about your diet, exercise, and sleep, ultimately improving your overall health. Here are some key reasons why you should consider using AI-enabled health and fitness apps:

- **Personalization**: Receive customized advice based on your unique health data and goals.
- **Automation**: Automatically track your activities, sleep, and nutrition without manual input.
- **Insights**: Gain deeper insights into your health patterns and behaviors.

How Do I Get Them?

Most AI-enabled health and fitness apps are available for download on smartphones and wearable devices. Here's how you can access some popular options:

MyFitnessPal: A comprehensive app for tracking nutrition and exercise.

- For further info go to: MyFitnessPal or https://www.myfitnesspal. com/

Sleep Cycle: An app designed to analyze and improve your sleep patterns.

- For further info go to: Sleep Cycle or https://www.sleepcycle.com/

Fitbit: A wearable fitness tracker that monitors physical activity, heart rate and sleep.

- For further info go to: Fitbit or https://www.fitbit.com/global/us/

home

Apple Watch: A versatile smartwatch that tracks fitness activities, heart rate, and more.

- For further info go to: Apple Watch or https://www.apple.com/wa tch/

How Do I Use Them?

Using AI-enabled health and fitness apps is straightforward. Here's a step-by-step guide:
MyFitnessPal:

Set Up: Download and open the MyFitnessPal app. Create an account and enter your health goals, such as weight loss, maintenance, or gain.
Tracking Nutrition:

- Log your daily meals by searching the extensive food database or scanning barcodes.
- MyFitnessPal will automatically calculate your calorie intake and macronutrient distribution.

Tracking Exercise:

- Log your workouts or connect the app to other fitness trackers to automatically sync your activity data.

Sleep Cycle:

- **Set Up**: Download and open the Sleep Cycle app. Create an account and grant necessary permissions for sleep tracking.

Improving Sleep Patterns:

- Place your phone near your bed and let Sleep Cycle monitor your sleep using sound analysis or accelerometer data.
- Review your sleep patterns and get personalized advice on how to improve your sleep quality.

Fitbit:

Set Up: Download and open the Fitbit app. Create an account and pair it with your Fitbit device.

Monitoring Physical Activity:

- Wear your Fitbit throughout the day to automatically track steps, heart rate, and sleep.
- Sync your data with the app to view detailed activity and health reports.

Apple Watch:

- **Set Up**: Pair your Apple Watch with your iPhone and install the necessary health and fitness apps.

Tracking Fitness:

- Use the built-in Workout app to track various exercises.
- Monitor your heart rate, activity levels, and sleep patterns with the Health app.

How Can They Save Me Time and Money?

AI-enabled health and fitness apps can significantly improve your efficiency and save you time and money. Here's how:

- **Time Savings**: Automate tracking of your nutrition, exercise, and sleep, reducing the time spent on manual logging.
- **Cost Savings**: Identify unhealthy spending habits on food and make informed decisions to reduce grocery bills. For instance, MyFitnessPal can help you track your grocery expenses and avoid unnecessary purchases.
- **Health Savings**: Prevent costly medical issues by maintaining a healthier lifestyle. Regular monitoring and personalized advice can help you avoid chronic conditions that lead to high medical expenses.

How Else Can They Benefit Me?

Beyond saving time and money, AI-enabled health and fitness apps offer several additional benefits:

- **Improved Health**: Receive personalized recommendations for diet, exercise, and sleep to enhance your overall health and well-being.

- **Motivation**: Track your progress and achieve milestones, which can motivate you to stay on track with your health goals.
- **Stress Reduction**: Automated tracking and personalized insights can reduce the stress associated with managing your health.

Practical Demo: Setting Up and Using AI-Enabled Health and Fitness Apps

To help you get started, let's walk through a practical demo of setting up and using AI-enabled health and fitness features in MyFitnessPal, Sleep Cycle, Fitbit, and Apple Watch:

MyFitnessPal Setup:

Log Meals:

- Open the MyFitnessPal app and go to the diary section.
- Tap on "Add Food" and search for your meal or scan the barcode.
- Enter the portion size and add it to your diary.

Sleep Cycle Setup:

Start Sleep Tracking:

- Open the Sleep Cycle app and set your wake-up window.
- Place your phone near your bed and start tracking.

Fitbit Setup:

Track Activity:

- Wear your Fitbit and ensure it is synced with the app.
- Open the app to view your steps, heart rate, and sleep data.

Apple Watch Setup:
Monitor Workouts:

- Open the Workout app on your Apple Watch.
- Select your workout type and start tracking.

AI-enabled health and fitness apps are powerful tools that allow you to prioritize your health in the simplest and easiest of ways. Not only do they highlight the areas of your life that need changes, they also motivate and encourage you as you make your way to a healthier way of living.

Building Block 6: AI Language Translation Tools

Meet Ali, Gabrielle, and Nikolai—three individuals from different parts of the world who have used AI-powered language translation tools to bridge communication gaps and enhance their travel experiences.

Ali, an American engineer, decided to take his family on a long-awaited vacation to Italy. Despite his basic knowledge of Italian, he was worried about navigating through the country, especially with young children in tow. Ali used Google Translate to assist with real-time communication. At restaurants, he simply spoke into his phone, and Google Translate provided instant Italian translations to the waitstaff. When visiting historical sites, Ali used the app's camera feature to take pictures of signs and plaques, instantly translating the Italian text into English. This feature not only helped his family understand the historical context but also made their travel experience richer and more enjoyable.

Gabrielle, a French marketing executive, traveled to Brazil for a business conference. Although she was fluent in French and English, Portuguese was a new challenge for her. Gabrielle relied on Microsoft Translator to communicate with local colleagues and clients. During meetings, she used the app's conversation mode, allowing her and her

Brazilian counterparts to speak into their devices and receive real-time translations. Additionally, Gabrielle used the app to translate presentation slides and documents, ensuring she could follow along and contribute effectively. The seamless communication facilitated by AI translation tools helped Gabrielle build stronger business relationships and navigate the conference with confidence.

Nikolai, a Norwegian student studying archaeology, visited Egypt for a research project. Arabic, the dominant language in Egypt, was unfamiliar to him. To overcome the language barrier, Nikolai turned to Google Translate. The app's voice translation feature allowed him to interact with locals and gather information about archaeological sites. He also used the camera translation feature to read museum exhibits and historical markers. By taking pictures of Arabic signs, Google Translate provided instant translations, enabling Nikolai to understand and document important information for his research. These tools made his academic journey in Egypt more productive and less stressful.

These stories highlight the transformative power of AI-powered language translation tools in overcoming language barriers and enhancing travel experiences. Let's explore how you can leverage these tools to improve your language skills and communication capabilities.

What are AI Language Translation Tools and Why Should I Use Them?

AI language translation tools use artificial intelligence and machine learning to translate text, speech, and images from one language to another. These tools can help you understand and communicate in languages you don't speak, making them incredibly useful for various situations. Here are some key reasons why you should consider using AI language translation tools:

- **Ease of Communication**: Overcome language barriers in real-time conversations.
- **Learning Aid**: Assist in learning new languages by providing accurate translations and pronunciation guides.
- **Travel Convenience**: Navigate foreign countries more easily with instant translations of signs, menus, and conversations.

How Do I Use Them?

Using AI language translation tools is straightforward. Here's a step-by-step guide:

Google Translate: https://translate.google.com

Text Translation:

- Open the Google Translate app and select the source and target languages.
- Enter the text you want to translate and view the translation

instantly.

Speech Translation

- Tap the microphone icon, speak into your device, and view the translated text.

Image Translation

- Tap the camera icon, point your camera at the text, and the app will translate it in real time.

Microsoft Translator: https://www.microsoft.com/en-us/translator

Set Up: Download and open the Microsoft Translator app. Choose the languages you want to translate between.

Text Translation:

- Enter the text you want to translate and receive an instant translation.

Voice Translation:

- Tap the microphone icon and speak; the app will translate your speech into the target language.

Conversation Mode:

- Use the conversation feature to translate real-time dialogues between speakers of different languages.

How Can They Save Me Time and Money?

AI language translation tools can significantly improve your efficiency and save you time and money. Here's how:

- **Time Savings**: Instant translations allow for quick understanding and communication, eliminating the need to manually look up words or phrases.
- **Cost Savings**: Avoid hiring human translators for basic communication needs. Apps like Google Translate and Microsoft Translator are free or low-cost compared to professional translation services.
- **Travel Efficiency**: Translate signs, menus, and conversations on the go, reducing the need for guided tours or translation services.

How Else Can They Benefit Me?

Beyond saving time and money, AI language translation tools offer several additional benefits:

- **Learning and Education**: Enhance your language learning process with accurate translations, pronunciation guides, and context understanding.
- **Accessibility**: Make content accessible to non-native speakers, improving inclusivity in various settings such as education, business,

and travel.

- **Convenience**: Easily switch between languages and use translation features offline in many apps, making them reliable tools in areas with limited internet access.

Practical Demo: Setting Up and Using AI Language Translation Tools

To help you get started, let's walk through a practical demo of setting up and using AI language translation features in Google Translate and Microsoft Translator:

Google Translate Setup
  Text Translation:

- Open the Google Translate app and select the source and target languages.
- Enter the text you want to translate and view the translation instantly.

Speech Translation in Google Translate:

- Tap the microphone icon and speak into your device.
- The app will translate your speech and display the translated text.

Image Translation in Google Translate:

- Tap the camera icon in the Google Translate app.

- Point your camera at the text you want to translate, and the app will overlay the translation on the image in real-time.

Microsoft Translator Setup
Conversation Mode:

- Open the Microsoft Translator app and select the conversation icon.
- Each participant selects their language, and the app translates spoken language in real-time.

AI language translation tools are incredibly powerful resources that can help you break down language barriers, making communication easier and traveling more enjoyable. As you begin to integrate these tools, you will find they open more opportunities into your life. Over time your appreciation for them will only grow.

Conclusion

As you made your way through these chapters you experienced how AI can transform your daily life in powerful and practical ways. From voice-activated assistants and AI-powered email management to smart navigation, financial management, and health and fitness tracking. AI tools can enhance efficiency, save time and money, and improve your overall quality of life.

Through integrating these building blocks into your life and with consistent and regular use of their tools, you will become more adept at leveraging their capabilities, leading to greater productivity and simplicity in your daily tasks.

With real-world examples and detailed instructions, you have been equipped with practical skills to begin to build your smart life with AI. Whether you're using Apple Watch to improve your health, Mint to track your finances, or Google Translate to communicate in different languages, the potential for AI to improve your life is immense.

The roles these building blocks play in your life will be dynamic as AI technology is constantly evolving, offering new tools and features to explore. Stay curious and keep experimenting with new AI solutions that can further enhance your productivity and simplify your life. As you do so, continue to come back to these chapters when you feel it is time to make lifestyle changes and reassess how these building blocks should be re-imagined in your routine.

As I write this conclusion, I feel the book itself is an introduction to a new phase of life- a phase where we and AI are reinventing our relationship with each other and how we interact.

During my college days, the world was technologically such a different place. We had not interacted with technology enough to clearly understand what was to come. I, for one, did not think my Computer Science professor's excitement around the idea that we can now send a letter via a computer would one day evolve to 'sending an email,' one of the most basic means of modern-day communication. Or my IT & Globalization professor's lecture about imagining a time where people can pick up a phone and call someone simply by saying their name will become one of the most basic features of a smartphone. These ideas seemed futuristic and Sci-fi at the time. We have now interacted enough with technology to know that what is being met with wonderment and disbelief today will soon become the most basic aspects of life.

With the current explosion of AI, I see two schools of thought. One is the group that views it with nervousness and trepidation while the other is going head on and practicing over consumption and extreme overuse.

And here again, I find myself advocating for the approach I have learnt to interact with technology and AI from – the safe and comfortable, almost nonchalant if you will, middle space. This is a time to be mindful and balanced when incorporating AI. Not too excited and not too afraid.

AI seems to be the shiny new object everyone feels is essential. The excitement of its potential coupled with the fear of falling behind can lead to other issues.

One of the risks is the over investment of time and resources. Fear driven adoption can result in spending on products and features that are fancy 'bells and whistles' with little to no value add. This is true in the business realms and it can be equally true in one's personal life.

As you start to build a smart life my hope is you will balance the type of AI you introduce into your life based on its value to your specific life and lifestyle. An intentional and mindful strategy will provide the necessary safeguards to ensure you truly live a smart life with AI.

With this conclusion, you've completed the journey through integrating the basic building blocks of AI into your daily routine. Not only have you laid the foundation of living a smart life with AI, but you have also embarked on the path to understanding the art of living with AI. Keep exploring, stay curious, and let AI be your companion in living a smarter, more joyful life.

If you would like to stay connected and learn more about adopting AI mindfully and effectively, visit https://qrco.de/bfHcfu or scan the QR Code at the end of this chapter and I will keep you up to date as I continue to design different areas of life and lifestyles with the building blocks of AI.

Scan to Stay Connected

Feedback

"Thousands of candles can be lit from a single candle, and the life of the candle will not be shortened. Happiness never decreases by being shared." – Buddha

When we share our experiences, we light the way for others, while spreading more happiness into the world. Let's brighten someone's journey together!

Would you help someone like you—curious about beginning a journey with Artificial Intelligence but unsure where to start?

Your review could help spark someone's discovery of AI and make a real difference.

To make a difference, simply scan the QR code below and leave a review:

Thank you for leaving a Review

Thank you for lighting the path and making the world a brighter and more beautiful place!

Misha Habib

References

Schwab, K. (2017). The Fourth Industrial Revolution. Crown Business.

Lee, K. (2018). AI Superpowers: China, Silicon Valley, and the New World Order. Houghton Mifflin Harcourt.

McKinsey & Company. (2018). AI Adoption Advances, But Foundational Barriers Remain. Retrieved from https://www.mckinsey.com/business-functions/mckinsey-analytics/our-insights/ai-adoption-advances-but-foundational-barriers-remain

PwC. (2017). Sizing the Prize: What's the Real Value of AI for Your Business and How Can You Capitalize? Retrieved from https://www.pwc.com/gx/en/issues/analytics/assets/pwc-ai-analysis-sizing-the-prize-report.pdf

Accenture. (2016). Why Artificial Intelligence is the Future of Growth. Retrieved from https://www.accenture.com/us-en/insight-artificial-intelligence-future-growth

OpenAI. (2024). ChatGPT: An AI Language Model. Retrieved from https://www.openai.com/research/chatgpt

Google Translate. (2024). Retrieved from https://translate.google.com

Microsoft Translator. (2024). Retrieved from https://www.microsoft. com/en-us/translator

Mint. (2024). Retrieved from https://www.mint.com

Wealthfront. (2024). Retrieved from https://www.wealthfront.com

Google Finance. (2024). Retrieved from https://www.google.com/ finance

Apple Wallet. (2024). Retrieved from https://www.apple.com/apple-pay/

Gmail Help. (2024). Filters and Blocked Addresses. Retrieved from https://support.google.com/mail/answer/6579?hl=en

Waze Help Center. (2024). Retrieved from https://support.google.com/ waze/answer/6268717?hl=en

Google Maps Help. (2024). Retrieved from https://support.google.co m/maps/answer/144349?hl=en

Uber Help. (2024). How to Request a Ride. Retrieved from https://hel p.uber.com/riders/article/how-to-request-a-ride?nodeId=6d23dc3a-2fe1-499e-9961-10dcf31a8f47

MyFitnessPal. (2024). Retrieved from https://www.myfitnesspal.com

Sleep Cycle. (2024). Retrieved from https://www.sleepcycle.com

Fitbit. (2024). Retrieved from https://www.fitbit.com

Apple Watch. (2024). Retrieved from https://www.apple.com/apple-watch/

Apple Inc. (2024). *Set up Siri on all your Apple devices.* Retrieved from https://support.apple.com/en-us/HT204389

Google Inc. (2024). *Set up and use Google Assistant.* Retrieved from https://support.google.com/assistant/answer/7172657

Amazon. (2024). *Set up Alexa on your Echo device.* Retrieved from https://www.amazon.com/gp/help/customer/display.html?nodeId=201602230

About the Author

Misha Habib holds a Master of Science in Analysis, Design, and Management of Information Systems from The London School of Economics & Political Science. With over 20 years of experience, she has introduced IT innovations across diverse sectors while living in nine cities spanning three continents. Since moving to California's Bay Area in 2016, Misha has worked at Fortune 500 companies, including Walmart.com (2016-2021) and Airbnb (2022-2024), driving rapid growth in IT and Artificial Intelligence.